EXPERIMENTS WITH SPORTS

A T R U E   B O O K®

by

Salvatore Tocci

Children's Press®
A Division of Scholastic Inc.

New York Toronto London Auckland Sydney
Mexico City New Delhi Hong Kong
Danbury, Connecticut

Reading Consultant
Susan Virgilio

Science Consultant
Tenley Andrews

The photo on the cover shows a tennis racket hitting a tennis ball. The photo on the title page shows a child hitting a tennis ball with a baseball bat.

The author and publisher are not responsible for injuries or accidents that occur during or from any experiments. Experiments should be conducted in the presence of or with the help of an adult. Any instructions of the experiments that require the use of sharp, hot, or other unsafe items should be conducted by or with the help of an adult.

Library of Congress Cataloging-in-Publication Data

Tocci, Salvatore.
   Experiments with sports / by Salvatore Tocci.
      p. cm. — (A true book)
   Summary: Explores the science behind sports through simple experiments using everyday objects.
Includes bibliographical references and index.
   ISBN 0-516-22789-0 (lib. bdg.)   0-516-27807-X (pbk.)
   1. Science—Experiments—Juvenile literature. 2. Sports—Experiments—Juvenile literature. [1. Science—Experiments. 2. Sports—Experiments. 3. Experiments.] I. Title. II. Series.
Q164.T676 2003
507.8—dc21

                            2002015262

CHILDREN'S PRESS, and A TRUE BOOK®, and associated logos are trademarks and or registered trademarks of Scholastic Library Publishing.
SCHOLASTIC and associated logos are trademarks and or registered trademarks of Scholastic Inc.
1 2 3 4 5 6 7 8 9 10 R 12 11 10 09 08 07 06 05 04 03

Contents

What's Your Favorite Sport?

Do you like to race against your friends to see who is the fastest? If you do, then your favorite sport may involve speed. In football, running backs and pass receivers must be fast to score touchdowns. In track, an athlete must run

even faster. To win the
100-meter dash, a world-class
runner must reach a speed of
more than 20 miles (32 kilo-
meters) per hour. In downhill
skiing, a world-class racer can
reach a speed of almost 140
miles (225 km) per hour!

Perhaps your favorite sport
involves balance. In hockey,
players must balance them-
selves on skates as they
speed along the ice. In soccer, players must keep their
balance as they use their feet

to move the ball down the field.

Perhaps your favorite sport involves accuracy. In basketball, players must shoot accurately to score points. In baseball, pitchers must throw accurately to strike out the batters.

Whether your favorite sport is football, track, skiing, hockey, soccer, basketball, or baseball, they all have something in common. As you will learn by doing the experiments in this book, all sports involve science.

Do You Need Speed?

If your favorite sport involves speed, it also involves **friction**. Friction is a force that can slow down and stop a moving object. Obviously, you do not want too much friction between your feet and the ground if you want to run fast. But if you have too little friction, you will slip and

Sneakers provide just the right amount of friction so that this basketball player can race down the court without slipping.

fall easily. Why are sneakers better to wear than leather-soled shoes for running fast without slipping?

Increasing Friction

You will need:
- pencil
- large paper cup
- sneaker
- smooth tabletop
- marbles
- leather-soled shoe (same size as the sneaker)

Use the pencil to punch two holes in the paper cup on opposite sides near the top. Undo the lace from the sneaker, except for the pair of holes closest to the toe. Knot each end of the lace through a hole in the paper cup. Place the sneaker on the table so that the cup hangs over the edge. Place a marble in the cup.

How many marbles must you put into the cup to get the sneaker to fall off the table? Repeat this experiment using the leather-soled shoe. How many marbles must you put in the cup this time?

Did you find that it took fewer marbles to drag the shoe off the table? You do not need as much force to move the

shoe. There is less friction between the shoe and the tabletop than there is between the sneaker and the tabletop, so the shoe slides more easily across the surface. For this reason, you would slide and

fall easily if you tried to run too fast in leather-soled shoes. Wearing sneakers creates just the right amount of friction so that you do not slip when you run fast.

Experiment with different types of athletic shoes to see which one produces the most friction. See how well these shoes slide across different types of surfaces, such as marble, wood, tile, and vinyl.

The less friction there is, the faster these hockey players can skate down the ice.

Unlike most athletes, hockey players and skiers want as little friction as possible between them and the ground so that they can move quickly across ice or snow. Athletes reduce friction in several ways. How can you reduce friction?

Experiment 2

Reducing Friction

You will need:
- two rulers or wood strips that are the same size
- aluminum foil
- tape
- several books
- table
- two quarters
- scissors
- plastic bag
- fabric with rough surface, such as burlap
- waxed paper

Cover one of the rulers or wood strips with aluminum foil and use tape to secure it. Stack the books on the table. Lean both rulers against the books to make slides. Tape the bottoms of the rulers to the table so they are even. Hold a quarter at the top of each ruler.

Release both quarters at the same time. Which quarter reaches the bottom first? If the foil reduces friction, the quarter sliding down the covered ruler should reach the bottom first. Remove the foil from the ruler and test the other materials, such as plastic, burlap, and waxed paper, to see

which ones reduce friction. Do any of the materials increase friction by slowing down the quarter? Now do you know why athletes put wax on their skates and skis? Do you know why skaters and skiers also crouch when they want to move fast?

Flying Like the Wind

You will need:
- two sheets of paper
- book

Crumple one piece of paper into a small ball. Hold the paper ball in one hand and the uncrumpled sheet of paper in your other hand in front of you. Release both papers at the same time. Which one hits the floor first? Next, hold the sheet of paper and the book in front of you. Which one hits the floor first when you release them? Now put the sheet of paper under the book and release them. What happens?

Finally, put the
piece of paper on top of
the book and release them.
Are you surprised by what
happens this time?

Even when it is on
top, the sheet of
paper will hit the
ground at the same
time as the book.

Although you cannot see them, the air is filled with tiny particles of gas. These gases include oxygen and carbon dioxide. Any object that moves through the air collides with these particles. As a result, these particles create **air resistance**. In other words, they slow down an object that is moving through the air.

The paper ball is more compact than the sheet of paper. For this reason, the paper ball collides with fewer particles and therefore meets less air resistance. As a result, it drops much faster than does the sheet of paper. Speed skaters move faster when they tuck in their arms and crouch low because they collide with fewer air particles.

You proba-
bly were not
surprised to
find that the
book hit the
floor before
the paper.
You also
probably
were not
surprised
to see
both of them

hit the floor at the same time when
the paper was underneath the book. But
you probably were surprised to find that
both of them hit the floor at the same

The leader collides with most of the air particles and moves them out of the way, making it easier for the other riders to pedal.

time when the paper was on top of the book. The paper appears to stick to the book as it falls. Actually, the book pushes away the particles in the air, clearing the way for the paper. Bicycle racers and runners help one another in the same way.

Do You Need Balance?

Some athletes crouch not because they want to avoid colliding with air particles, but because they want to keep their balance. For example, one reason why baseball batters crouch with their feet apart is to keep their balance when they hit the ball. Football players crouch when they line up so that they don't get knocked over when they are hit.

Other athletes twist their bodies to keep their balance. For example, gymnasts must know exactly how to twist their bodies to remain on a balance beam while performing a routine.

What all these athletes are doing is changing their **centers of gravity**. The center of gravity is the point on which an object can balance itself. Every object

has a center of gravity, but it is not always located in the center of the object.

Experiment 4

Finding the Center of Gravity

You will need:
- modeling clay
- yardstick

Squeeze a small ball of clay around one end of the yardstick. Support the yardstick and clay by placing a finger from each hand on either end. Slowly slide your fingers together, making sure that the yardstick does not fall.

At some point, your fingers will come together with the yardstick balanced on top of them. Repeat this experiment several times, moving the spot where you place the

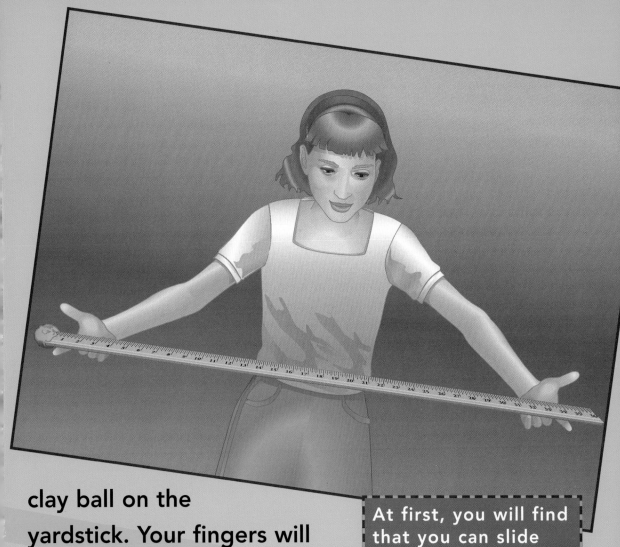

clay ball on the yardstick. Your fingers will always meet at the yardstick's center of gravity. Where is your center of gravity?

At first, you will find that you can slide one finger faster than the other. Then your other finger will slide faster.

Experiment 5

Finding Your Center of Gravity

You will need:
- thick pillow
- chair
- an adult helper

Place the pillow over the back of the chair. Ask an adult to hold the chair while you try to balance yourself on the back of it so that your body is parallel to the ground. Where is the chair touching your body when you are

This high jumper's center of gravity is actually a point that is outside his body.

balanced? This point is your center of gravity. The human body is not flat like a yardstick, so your center of gravity is actually halfway through your body at this point. However, your center of gravity is not always in the same spot. It can change when you move your arms and legs. What happens when your center of gravity changes?

Experiment 6

Falling Over

You will need:
- empty 2-liter plastic soda bottle with cap
- table
- sink

Fill the bottle with tap water and cap it tightly. Stand the bottle on the table. Tilt the bottle slightly, supporting it with your finger on the cap. Remove your finger. What happens to the bottle? Pour some of the water from the bottle into the sink and then repeat the experiment. Keep pouring water out of the bottle until it no longer falls over when you release it.

If an object has a high center of gravity, it can fall over easily. The more water the

bottle contains, the higher its center of gravity. This is why the bottle falls over easily when it is full. By removing some water, you lower the bottle's center of gravity. When the center of gravity is low enough, the bottle can balance itself after you remove your finger.

If the bottle is full of water, it will fall over when you release it.

By bending their knees, baseball players lower their centers of gravity. By lowering their centers of gravity, they are less likely to lose their balance when they swing hard at the ball. If they keep their balance, they are more likely to hit the ball with their bat at just the right spot. If the batter hits it at just the right spot, the ball may travel far enough for the batter to score a home run.

Do You Need Accuracy?

To hit a home run, a batter needs more than just power. A batter must also hit the ball at just the right spot on the bat. Baseball players call this the "sweet spot." Hitting the ball with the sweet spot transfers most of the power from the batter to the ball. How can you find out where the sweet spot is?

Hitting a Baseball

You will need:
• baseball bat
• helper
• hammer
• tape

Curl your fingertips around the knob of the bat. Let the bat hang straight down. Ask someone to tap the bat with the hammer near the knob. Can you feel the vibrations in your fingertips?

Have a helper continue tapping the bat, each time moving down a little bit. At some point, you should not feel any vibrations. Mark this spot with a piece of tape.

Ask the person to continue tapping his or her way down the bat. You should start to feel the vibrations again. The tape marks the bat's sweet spot.

When you hit a ball, the power from your swing causes vibrations to move up and down the bat. In other words, much of the power goes into the bat and not the ball. But if you hit the ball with the sweet spot, the vibrations travel up and down the bat in a different way. They cancel one another so you don't feel them. In this case, most of your power goes to the ball rather than the bat.

Now that you know about the science of hitting a baseball, find out about the science of throwing a football.

Baseball players know when they hit the ball on the bat's sweet spot because their hands don't feel the bat vibrating.

Throwing a Football

You will need:
- measuring tape
- chalk
- outdoor brick or concrete wall
- football

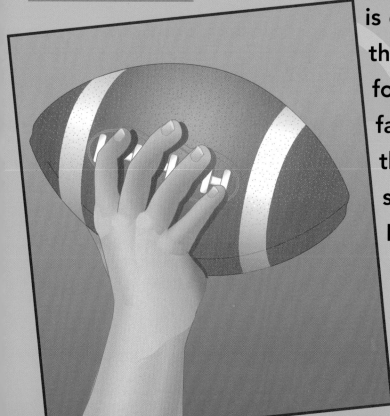

Use the chalk to draw a 3-foot (1-m) square on the wall. Stand 5 ft. (1.5 m) in front of the square. Hold the football so that your hand is centered around the middle of the football at its fattest spot. Throw the football at the square ten times. How many times did you hit the target?

Try hitting the target again, this time standing 10 ft. (3 m) from the wall. How many times did you hit it this time? Keep moving back 5 ft. (1.5 m) each time until you no longer can hit the wall. What happens to your accuracy as you keep moving back?

Repeat the experiment, again starting 5 ft. (1.5 m) from the target. This time, how-ever, hold the football the way a quarterback holds it. Place your hand around the ball so that your index finger touches the end of the laces. How does throwing the football this way affect your accuracy? Can you throw it farther when you hold the football the way a quarterback holds it?

When you hold the football around its fattest part, you are holding it around its

center of gravity. Throwing the ball this way causes it to float through the air. When you hold the football the way a quarterback holds it, you are holding it behind its center of gravity. Throwing the ball this way causes it to spiral. You can be more accurate and throw a football farther when you make it spiral. How should you shoot a basketball to be accurate and get it through the basket?

Shooting a Basketball

You will need:
- basketball
- basket

Stand a few feet from the basket. Shoot the basketball ten times from three different angles. Which angle gives you the best accuracy? If you watch a basketball game, you will notice that the players do not shoot the ball from either a low angle or from a high angle. They shoot the basketball from an angle somewhere in between the two. The basketball is more likely to enter the basket at this angle.

Shoot the basketball from three different angles. First, shoot it straight at the basket. Then, shoot it at an angle. Finally, shoot it by aiming high.

Fun With Sports

Knowing about friction can give you the speed you need in football, track, or skiing. Knowing about the center of gravity can help you keep your balance in hockey, soccer, or gymnastics. Knowing how to hit or throw a ball can help you be accurate in baseball,

football, or basketball. Knowing
about the science of sports
can even help you impress your
family and friends with a trick.

Experiment 10

Staying in Place

You will need:
- small table
- place mat
- small sports-related item, such as a baseball cap or swimming goggles

Place the table outdoors. Set the place mat on the table. Place the object on the place mat. Grab the place mat with both hands and pull it straight out from under the object as quickly as you can. If you're quick enough, the object should stay on the table.

An object will not move unless some kind of force, such as a push or pull, is applied to it. This resistance to moving is called **inertia**. The object remains on the table because of inertia.

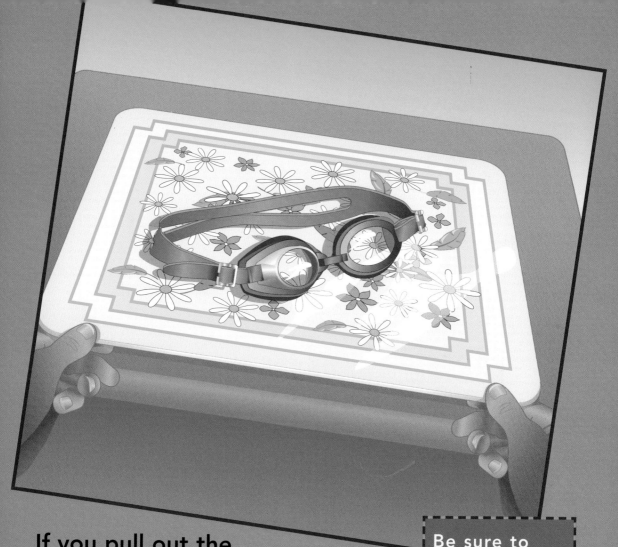

If you pull out the
place mat quickly enough, little
force is transferred to the object.
The object remains on the table.

Be sure to
pull the place
mat straight
out in one
quick motion.

To Find Out More

If you would like to learn more about the science of sports, check out these additional resources.

 **Books**

Barr, George. **Sports Science for Young People.** Dover Publications, 1991.

Davis, Susan. **The Sporting Life.** Henry Holt, 1997.

Gardner, Robert. **Health Science Projects About Sports Performance.** Enslow Publishers, 2002.

Goodstein, Madeline. **Sports Science Projects: The Physics of Balls in Motion.** Enslow Publishers, 1999.

Wiese, Jim. **Sports Science: 40 Goal-Scoring, High-Flying, Medal-Winning Experiments for Kids.** John Wiley & Sons, 2002.

Organizations and Online Sites

Bayer Rubber
http://www.bayerrubberus.com/bayerrubberus/KidsPage.nsf

Carry out the experiment titled "The Tail of Two Rubbers" to understand the difference between a super-ball, a tennis ball, and a golf ball, all of which are made of rubber.

Exploratorium
3601 Lyon Street
San Francisco, CA 94123
http://www.exploratorium.edu

This site helps you explore the science of baseball, skateboarding, hockey, and cycling. You can learn how to throw a fastball, curve-ball, screwball, and slider. The science behind each type of pitch is explained.

Hit-the-Dot
http://faculty.washington.edu/chudler/java/dottime.html

All sports require fast responses to situations that develop suddenly. Test your reaction time by clicking on the black dots as they appear in the white circles. Find out how many dots you can hit in thirty seconds.

10 Ways Exercise Helps You Focus in Class
http://www.kidsrunning.com/columns/attentionchecklist.html

Learn how jogging, skate-boarding, and squeezing a rubber ball can help you with your schoolwork.

Important Words

air resistance the ability of air to slow down a moving object

center of gravity the point on which an object can balance itself

friction a force that slows down and eventually stops a moving object

inertia the ability of an object that is not moving to remain in place, or the ability of an object that is moving to keep moving unless a push, a pull, or some other kind of force acts on it

Index

Meet the Author

Salvatore Tocci is a science writer who lives in East Hampton, New York, with his wife, Patti. He was a high school biology and chemistry teacher for almost thirty years. As a teacher, he always encouraged his students to perform experiments to learn about science. Whenever he goes downhill skiing, he tries to keep his center of gravity as low as possible.